# SCIENTIFIC VISUALIZATION

## THE NEW EYES OF SCIENCE

### CHRISTOPHER W. BAKER

NEW CENTURY
TECHNOLOGY

THE MILLBROOK PRESS
BROOKFIELD, CONNECTICUT

Cover image: A model of the results of one impact made when pieces of the comet P/Shoemaker-Levy 9 crashed into Jupiter in 1994. Courtesy of Dr. Mordecai-Mark Mac Low, American Museum of Natural History.

Photos courtesy of: Dr. Adam Burrows, Dept. of Astronomy, University of Arizona: pp. 4, 6; Prof. D.F. Coker/ Glenn Bresnahan, Boston University: p. 7; EECS Dept., M.I.T./ Brigham and Women's Hospital: pp. 8, 9, 10; M.I.T. Brain Atlas Project: p. 11; Center for Human Simulation, University of Colorado: p. 12; University of Maryland Chaos Group: p. 13; Mark Feighner/G. Bodvarsson, Earth Sciences Div./Wes Bethel, Visualization Group, Lawrence Berkeley National Lab: p. 15; David H. Laidlaw/Matthew J. Avalos/Russell E. Jacobs, Caltech Biological Imaging Center: p. 16; Prof. Charles Delisi/ Erik Brisson, Boston University: p. 17; Los Alamos National Laboratories: pp. 18, 23; Guangua Gao/Tahir Cagin/William Goddard, Caltech: p. 21; Ken Downing, Life Sciences Div./Wes Bethel, Visualization Group, Lawrence Berkeley National Lab: p. 22; Teresa Head-Gordon, Life Sciences Div./Terry Ligocki, Visualization Group, Lawrence Berkeley National Lab: p. 25; National Center for Supercomputing Applications, University of Illinois at Urbana-Champaign: pp. 26, 28, 31; NASA: pp. 30, 44; K. Droegemeier/M. Xue, CAPS, University of Oklahoma/G. Foss, Pittsburgh Supercomputing Center: p. 33 (top); Environmental and Societal Impacts Group, National Center for Atmospheric Research: p. 33 (bottom); NOAA/ERL Climate Diagnostics Center: p. 35; Paul Carlson: pp. 36, 37; Dept. of Nuclear Medicine, University of Buffalo School of Medicine and Biomedical Engineering: pp. 38, 43; Dept. of Computer Science, University of North Carolina: p. 39; Dr. V.F. Humphrey, Dept. of Physics, University of Bath, U.K.: p. 40; Dr. Robert C. Waag, Cornell Theory Center, Cornell University: p. 41; P.E.T. Center, Wake Forest University Baptist Medical Center: p. 42.

Library of Congress Cataloging-in-Publication Data
Baker, Christopher W.
Scientific visualization: the new eyes of science / Christopher W. Baker.
p. cm. — (New century technology)
Includes bibliographical references and index.
Summary: Describes the nature of scientific visualization and its use by scientists and doctors to interpret data and observe phenomena which were thought unobservable.
ISBN 0-7613-1351-6 (lib. bdg.)
1. Science—Methodology—Juvenile literature. 2. Visualization—Juvenile literature. 3. Digital computer simulation—Juvenile literature. [1. Science—Methodology. 2. Visualization. 3. digital computer simulation.] I. Title. II. Series.
Q175 .B164    2000    507.2—dc21                                             99-044812

Published by The Millbrook Press, Inc.
2 Old New Milford Road, Brookfield, Connecticut 06804    www.millbrookpress.com

# SCIENTIFIC VISUALIZATION

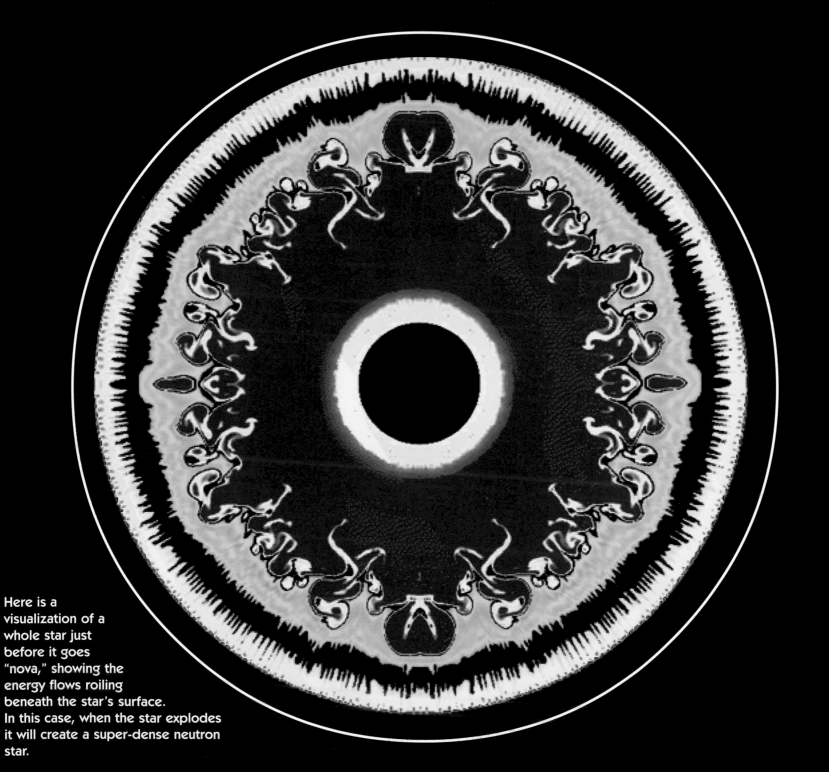

Here is a visualization of a whole star just before it goes "nova," showing the energy flows roiling beneath the star's surface. In this case, when the star explodes it will create a super-dense neutron star.

The massive red star before you is dying. Millions of years have passed since you saw it form, then grow, and now start to decay. In its final stages, the star's diameter has swollen to nearly a hundred million miles across. It would reach more than halfway to Earth from the position of our Sun, consuming Mercury, Venus, and our home planet with its heat.

You can see that the end is near. The star's hydrogen fuel has long been consumed, fused into helium, which in turn became carbon, oxygen, and finally iron at the core, roiling at a temperature above six billion degrees Fahrenheit.

Suddenly, the moment arrives. In less than a second, the core of the stellar giant collapses in a massive explosion, throwing off the light energy of a billion suns. The red outer shell is torn to shreds, blasting outward into surrounding space at more than 6,000 miles (9,656 kilometers) per second.

5

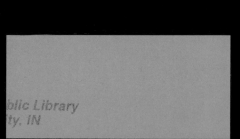

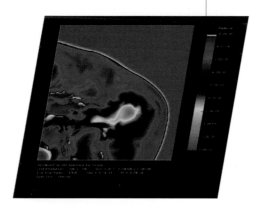

**A supernova is brewing. This image is part of a simulation visualizing the destruction of a star. It shows a section of a star's surface and the forces building up underneath.**

The fierce, explosive shock waves pulse inward as well, smashing the already condensing core in upon itself. If the surviving core is between one and three times the mass of our sun it will become a neutron star, an object so dense that a single tablespoon scooped from its surface would weigh about 50 billion tons on Earth.

But if it is more than three times larger than our Sun, as this star is, its collapse cannot be stopped. You watch as the implosion accelerates, pulling everything in upon itself until, suddenly, the star disappears altogether. Only blackness remains—a black hole in the universe where gravity is so intense that not even light can escape. . . .

Pulling your gaze from the monitor, you realize you have just witnessed the formation of a black hole, the end of a star's life and one of the most cataclysmic events in the entire universe. It is an event that no human has ever seen in person, nor likely will ever see.

## SEEING WITH NEW EYES

It is true that astronomers have viewed parts of a star's lengthy evolution by gazing through their telescopes on Earth and in space, but the only way anyone will see the entire life of a star, from its formation through its ultimate collapse, is on a computer.

It is this ability of computers to visualize what can't be experienced, and even what can hardly be imagined, that is changing science and our understanding of the world around us. This process is called scientific visualization.

The name itself is a mouthful. Could it be as complicated as it sounds? The answer is both yes and no. Simply said, scientific visualization is a fancy term for making pictures on the computer from scientific data or scientific theory. It doesn't matter where the data come from: a magnetic resonance imager (MRI) in a hospital, a set of buoys measuring ocean currents off the coast of South America, or a new theoretical computer simulation designed to predict the weather. The results can all be turned into an image of some sort that can help a scientist better understand a complex experiment or the latest theory.

Making pictures is the easy part to understand. The difficult and complex part is understanding exactly how this is done. And in scientific visualization, it is extremely important that the image created accurately reflects the data that are being analyzed.

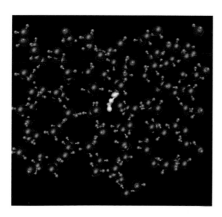 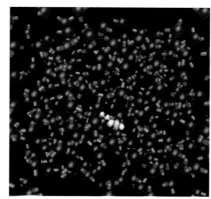

These two images were part of a study to test how hydrogen molecules move through water and ice. The hydrogen is shown in white. Note how the water molecules are farther apart in ice than in water. Water is one of the few fluids that expands when it turns into a solid.

Using an MRI scan as an example, we can see how the visualization process works. A patient lies down on the bed of an MRI scanner. The bed is then slowly moved into and through a large ring of magnets. The magnets produce an intense magnetic field, which affects the cells in a very thin slice of the patient's body. The results of this effect on the millions of cells in the slice is then sensed by the machine, and the data are stored on a computer. The scanner then moves the patient very slightly and scans another slice, until the entire area the doctor wants a picture of has been scanned.

The patient then returns to the hospital room, and the doctors are left with a huge amount of data to analyze. To understand the data, they could take each individual slice, put it on film, and look at it on a light box the way a dentist looks at X rays of your teeth. But what would they be looking at? A whole wall of individual pictures would be difficult to understand.

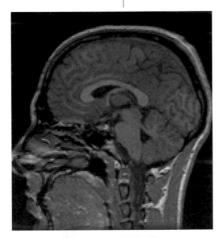

**A single MRI slice**

A better way to view the data would be to somehow stack all of these images on top of one another and make one big image to explore. This is actually what the MRI's computer does automatically for the doctors. It not only stacks the data slices, but it also colors each type of tissue differently and displays the results on the computer screen. Skin, for example, can look pinkish, while the skull underneath looks white, and the brain beneath the skull, gray. Other colors can be chosen as well if the doctors think they will provide a clearer image.

## No Matter How You Slice It

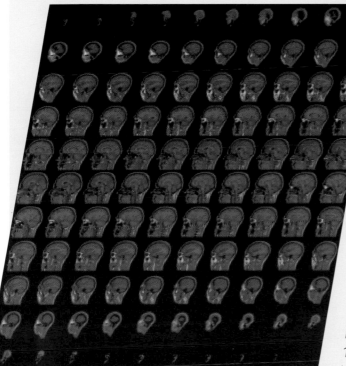

This image shows a full series of MRI slices progressing from one side of a patient's head to the other. It is much easier to understand the information presented when all the slices are combined into a single 3-D image.

*Try to imagine just how complicated it might be to understand what all those separate image slices could mean. An MRI slice can vary from 3 millimeters to about 8 millimeters, depending on what part of the body is being imaged.*

*In the brain, because of the need for increased precision, a slice the size of 3 millimeters is most often used. Look on any ruler that has both centimeters and inches. Find the 10-centimeter mark and the 11-centimeter mark. In between those are ten little lines, each one millimeter apart. Three of those make up one MRI slice.*

*For your head and neck alone, there could be more than 50 MRI pictures to look at. (MRI systems usually leave about 1 millimeter of free space between the MRI images themselves.) An ultrafine MRI slice was used in the image to the left, resulting in over 100 separate images. No matter how you slice it, that's a lot of data!*

Doctors at Boston's Brigham and Women's Hospital use MRI visualization for pre-surgical planning. Here we see a fully-visualized brain with a tumor pointed out by the blue arrow as well as the crossed lines on the 2-D slices. The actual brain operation is shown in the upper-left corner.

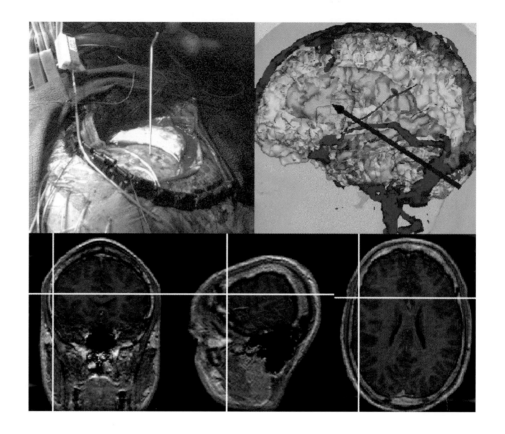

The doctors can now use the computer to cut away parts of this virtual skull and brain to find a suspected tumor, for example. What's more, they can turn and move the computer image of their patient's head any way they want, looking at the tumor from the bottom, top, or sides. This allows them to precisely locate, diagnose, and plan their upcoming treatment. Now you can begin to see why accuracy is so important.

# IT'S WHAT'S INSIDE
## THAT COUNTS

Just how is it that we can see what's inside the MRI image of the patient's head? It seems like magic, but it's really the result of a huge number of mathematical calculations. When the MRI has finished its scan, it has provided the computer with millions of points of information grouped together in a shape that looks like a patient's head.

This shape is then automatically divided up into millions of tiny cubes called voxels. You may not have heard of voxels, but you probably know something about pixels. Pixels are the tiny rectangles that make up the image on your computer screen. The smaller the pixels, the more there are on the screen, and thus the greater detail you can see in the image.

The same is true for voxels, except that they exist in three dimensions. If you think of the patient's head as one large cube, and then imagine cutting that cube into millions of tiny cubes, you will begin to understand what a voxel is.

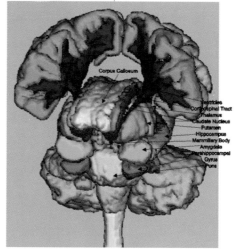

**Constructed from MRI data, this image of the human brain now serves as an important teaching tool.**

Inside each voxel lies one or perhaps many points of information gathered from the MRI scan. This information tells the computer something about the properties (density and cell type, for example) of the living cells in that area of the patient's head.

The University of Colorado's Visible Human Project created detailed models of the human body from MRI scans of actual human cadavers. The use of voxels to represent the data means that researchers can strip off the outer muscles and see the bones beneath, or even move their point of view into the lung cavity (the hollow part at the top of the image) to look at the torso from the inside.

## My Voxel Is Better Than Your Pixel

*Whether a pixel or a voxel is better to use in a visualization depends entirely on your data and how you want to view it. In the MRI example, voxels are essential because your data represent a 3-dimensional volume, and what is inside that volume (bones, nerves, and muscle tissue) is important to see. There are many cases, however, where simple pixels work better.*

*Visualizing mathematical equations, such as fractals, is one example. Fractals are equations that produce infinitely repetitive shapes and patterns of often astonishing beauty. Since mathematicians are often more interested in the surface shapes of equations than what lies inside, visualizing them with a computer does not require 3-dimensional voxels at all. Pixels work perfectly.*

Born from the field of study called chaos mathematics, this image shows what a particular fractal equation looks like. Note how the lines curve. They are bending around two specific areas called "strange attractors."

This information is processed, and based on the results, the computer assigns a color to that voxel. This series of calculations is repeated for each of the voxels that make up the shape being studied. The greater the number of voxels, the more calculations required, and the greater the resulting detail of the final image—just as it is with pixels.

Because brain cells share similar properties with each other, and tumor and bone cells have distinct properties that set them apart, the computer can create an image that shows the detailed inner structure of the brain and head. And since the voxels are 3-dimensional like a brick, for example, it doesn't matter whether the doctors look at the image from the top, sides, or bottom. They will always have a correct and accurate view.

Without this level of accuracy when visualizing a patient's brain, doctors might make an incorrect diagnosis, or perhaps even operate in the wrong area. While not all scientific visualizations involve such immediate life-and-death situations, accuracy is always a top priority.

In the Yucca Mountain area in Nevada, for example, underground rock formations are being studied as possible storage sites for nuclear waste. Geologists and hydrologists (scientists who study water) have taken drilling samples and done seismic tests to see if they can predict how groundwater flows through the area. If their visualizations of the data are not accurate, they may inadvertently pollute the underground water supply for hundreds of years to come, damaging the wildlife and making large areas around the mountain uninhabitable.

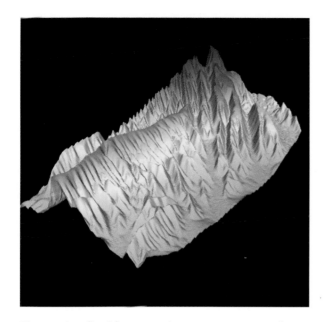 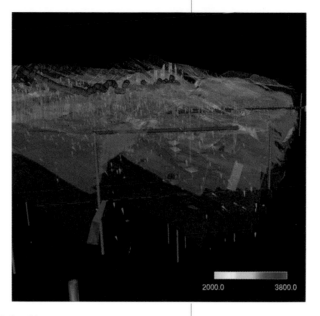

2000.0      3800.0

**These detailed images show an accurate picture of the Yucca Mountain terrain, as well as the water flows and various rock layers beneath the surface.**

## WHY GO TO ALL THIS TROUBLE?

Science, it seems, is continually building ever more expensive machines, such as miles-long atomic accelerators to study the smallest particles of nature, giant mountaintop telescopes to study the largest structures of the universe, or reusable spacecraft, like the space shuttle, to better understand our own planet and solar system. Why?

15

Talk about a sense of well bee-ing. Scientists at the California Institute of Technology use their micro MRI scanner to image a honeybee.

Essentially, it is because science is about extending our perception and thus our understanding of the universe in which we live. Each new tool of science, from the electron microscope to the Hubble space telescope, has done just that.

Anything that can give scientists a better grasp of their areas of research may possibly lead to a breakthrough in our understanding of who we are and where we came from.

This idea is at the heart of why scientific visualization is so vital. It is a tool so powerful that it is accelerating discovery in every area of science it touches. The saying "A picture is worth a thousand words" barely conveys its true power. Scientific visualization is not only worth a thousand words, but years of research time, millions of dollars saved, and untold numbers of lives made better.

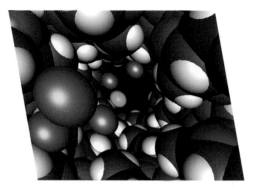

**Scientists at Boston University use a computer to watch how cell membrane channels function. These ion channels, as they are called, serve as gateways between the inside and outside of our bodies' cells and allow the movement of only certain kinds of molecules across the cell boundary. Here the protein structure of the channel is shown in red, gray, and white, while the ions in transit are blue and green.**

## EXTENDING PERCEPTION

Let's try a thought experiment to see if we can discover how using the computer to make pictures might actually help us. We'll start by frying an egg. But before we begin, let's become aware of the world that immediately surrounds us.

Sniff the air. If it's springtime and the windows are open, you might smell the flowers outside mixed with the scent of butter melting in the frying pan and the bread toasting in the toaster. What are you touching? The handle of the frying pan may be getting warm. Or maybe you are just putting it on the stove and the weight presses against your grip.

All around you are sounds, as well. Perhaps the toaster is popping up, the refrigerator motor is running, or the faucet is dripping.

And finally, what can you see? Out the window may be the green of the lawn while in front of you is the stove. As you turn, you can see the entire kitchen set up with its cupboards, appliances, and countertops.

**Have you ever looked closely at oil and vinegar salad dressing after shaking the bottle? The two fluids swirl around one another but never really mix. This image shows the dynamic action that takes place when oil and water come together.**

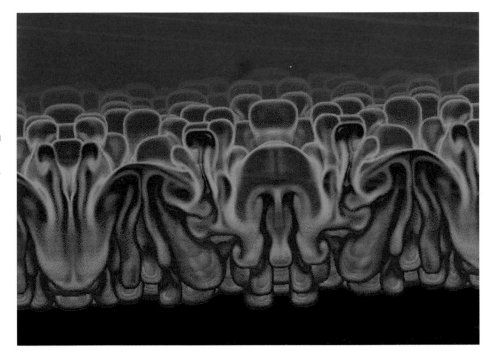

This is your world, the one that immediately surrounds you. It is all you can perceive. Can you smell, through the ceiling above, the wood of the rafters holding up the roof? Can you feel the iron molecules buried inside the frying-pan handle? Can you see into the dirt beneath the lawn, and inside the worms as they slowly enrich the earth? These are silly questions—of course you can't. Your senses, as rich as they may be, are limited. And it is this limitation, of vision in particular, that scientific visualization promises to expand.

## LET'S GET COOKING

Now let's fry our egg and pretend we are a food scientist who wants to understand why eggs sometime stick to frying pans. Let's concentrate on what we can observe as we cook. If you melted butter in the pan first, you can see some of it pushed aside as the egg drops onto the surface of the pan. You may notice that some of the egg has landed on the buttered part of the skillet, while some did not.

Depending on how hot the pan is, the clear part of the egg starts to cook and turns white until you can no longer see the pan beneath it. Finally, the time comes to serve the egg. The spatula slides easily underneath the buttered part, but where there was no butter, the egg sticks to the pan and tears. Whatever didn't stick to the skillet goes onto a plate, the burner is shut off, and the pan goes into the sink.

It's all so simple. Maybe you've done this dozens of times before. But what did we learn this time as a scientist? We know that heat cooks eggs and that direct contact with the metal of the pan makes them stick. Why this is so, however, is still a mystery.

## START YOUR IMAGINATION!

Let's imagine that we can get really small, about the size of an ant. We are so small, in fact, that we can stand on top of the newly cracked egg. The surface of the egg is very squishy, and our feet sink in a bit. As the egg cooks, the white becomes firmer and easier to stand on. Finally, we don't sink in at all.

The egg is now cooked. We had a close-up view, but did this tell us anything that we didn't know before? Once again, not really. This view didn't show us anything that we couldn't have seen with our own eyes at actual size.

Now it's time to get even smaller, way smaller. Let's shrink down well past what we can see with the unaided eye, down to the size of a molecule, and actually go inside the egg. When the egg is first cracked, it runs and flows like thick, somewhat sticky water. From your viewpoint inside the egg, you can see why this is so by looking at the egg proteins and other molecules that surround you. They are very loosely connected to one another, or maybe not connected at all. This allows them to easily roll and slide over and past one another as the egg flows onto the pan. They glide easily over the surface of the pan, too.

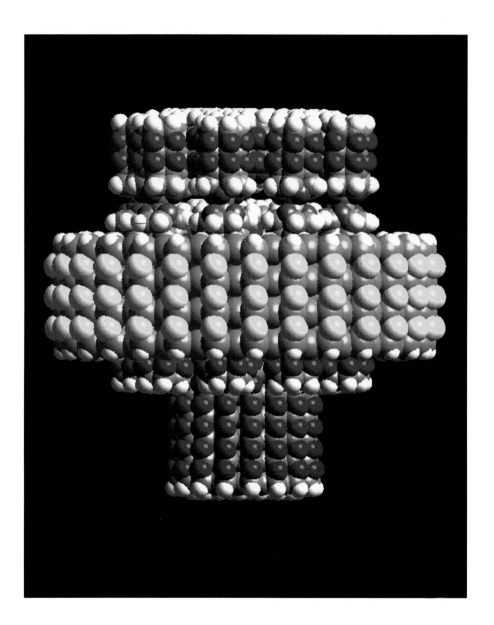

Nanotechnology is about building things out of single atoms and molecules. Here we see a visualization of what is called the Molecular Planetary Gear.

21

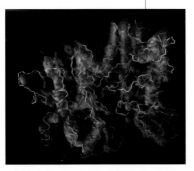

Molecules' shapes can tell chemists quite a bit about molecular behavior. The yellow tubelike structure shows the bends and turns of a molecule, and the semi-transparent rounded surfaces indicate the atoms the molecule is made up of.

As the heat cooks the egg, however, you start to notice some changes. The free-moving molecules begin to get more energetic, unraveling and tangling with one another forcefully and sometimes getting stuck together. The hotter it gets, the more places that egg molecules stick to one another, gradually losing their ability to move around so freely. We can also see that this same molecular sticking process is happening between the pan and the egg in the areas where there is no butter.

Additionally, all these new connections between the egg's molecules begin to fill in the more open areas around us, gradually blocking the light until we can no longer see out. To the outside viewer the liquid egg has just turned white.

## EVEN SMALLER?

We have learned something new by seeing our egg at the molecular level. It's like looking at a section of the egg through a high-powered microscope in a biology lab. Yet, even though molecules are quite small, there is a lot going on that we still can't see. We need to get even smaller to discover what else is going on when an egg gets cooked. To get to where the real action is, we need to shrink to the atomic level and look directly at the millions of atoms that make up the egg.

At this level we see energy (heat) coming into the egg system, causing its atoms to move around more rapidly and the electrons

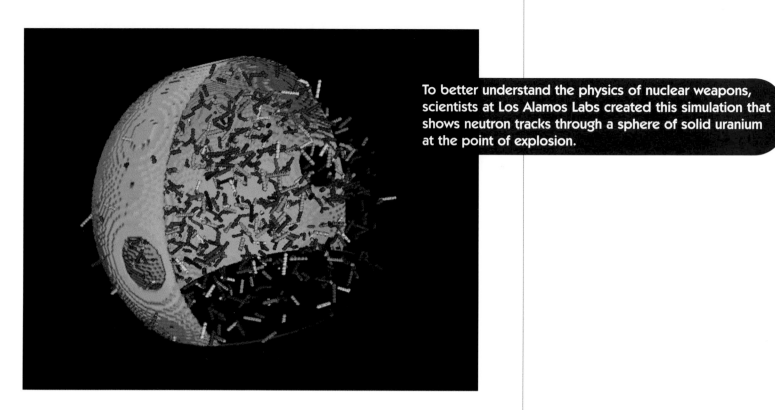

**To better understand the physics of nuclear weapons, scientists at Los Alamos Labs created this simulation that shows neutron tracks through a sphere of solid uranium at the point of explosion.**

surrounding these atoms to get more excited, throwing them into higher energy orbits around the nucleus. Some electrons may get so energized that they leave their atoms altogether, while others may actually become shared by two different atoms, linking them tightly together.

This and other forms of atomic bonding happens within the egg itself and between the egg and whatever molecules are close to it. Where the egg meets the frying pan, for example, the egg's molecules bond with the iron of the pan. The greater the heat in these areas, the more egg atoms bond with the pan and the greater the sticking.

These bonds can be quite strong. We know this from experience by the amount of heat (in the form of hot water), force (in the form of scrubbing or scraping), and solvents (in the form of dish soap) that we need in order to break these bonds and clean the egg off the pan.

And you thought you were just an average person making a quick breakfast! Our visualization has shown us that what you really are is a nuclear scientist and a chemist pushing atoms and molecules around so they connect with one another and form a solid out of a liquid. Scientific visualization uses a computer to achieve similar goals.

In the process, you also discovered why eggs stick to un-oiled frying pans. Though this is a simple example, it illustrates the process of discovery that scientists experience when they use scientific visualization to understand whatever it is they are studying.

## BEYOND TIME

Our ability to perceive and understand our world, however, is not only limited by the sizes of the things we wish to see, such as the atoms and molecules in the egg example above. It is also limited by our ability to perceive time. What is time? Time can be thought of as the interval between two sequential events. The space between two consecutive drumbeats is an example.

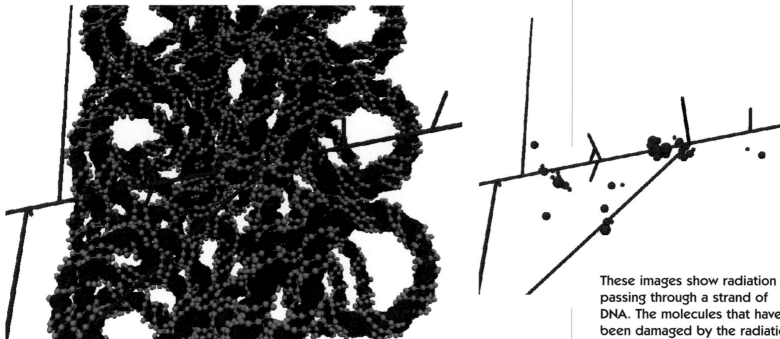

These images show radiation passing through a strand of DNA. The molecules that have been damaged by the radiation are shown in red. Since it is difficult to see exactly which molecules have been affected, the computer allows the researcher to look at just the radiation path and the damage it has caused.

Take a pencil, a spoon, or even a real drumstick and tap on a desk or tabletop. Tap twice, with one second in between the taps. You can time it with a watch or say "one Mississippi" in between taps. The empty space between taps represents about one second. A second is easy to perceive. How about a half a second? It's still not too hard to perceive, is it?

Now let's cut that second by ten. Or better yet, by a hundred. This time lapse is far more difficult to relate to. But we have all seen tenths of seconds and even hundredths of seconds ticking away furiously during Olympic sporting events like the bobsled run, where tiny amounts of time separate victory from defeat. Because of this, though the numbers are often a blur on the TV screen, we can still somehow relate to hundredths of a second.

But what if we go well beyond that to millionths of a second or billionths of a second, also known as nanoseconds? A nanosecond is so small that light, the fastest-moving energy in the universe, covers only about 1 foot (30 centimeters) in that amount of time. And what about a time interval many times smaller than that? A femtosecond, for example, is a thousandth of a trillionth of a second.

The point is that these amounts of time are so small that we can't possibly perceive anything that happens during such intervals. Yet important things do happen. Many molecular bonds break and form that quickly. Subatomic fission and fusion take place. In fact, according to physicist Stephen Hawking, the initial stages of our entire universe formed in even less time than a femtosecond.

How is it possible for us to ever know what is going on if we can't perceive it? Before scientific visualization was developed, scientists used complex mathematical equations to try to describe what was happening. But even for highly trained scientists, these could sometimes be difficult to relate to.

In this computer visualization of a black hole moving through space, we can see how the intense gravity forces actually distort the fabric of space time surrounding the hole.

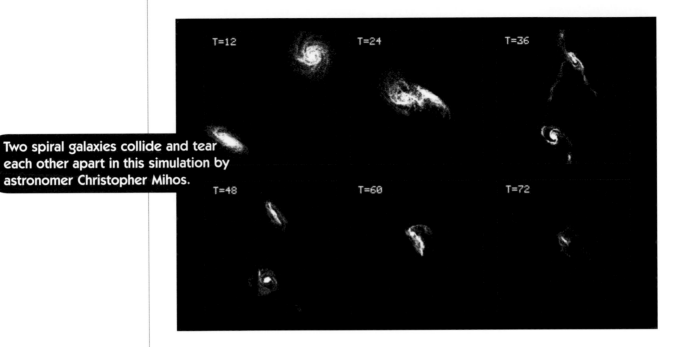

T=12        T=24        T=36

T=48        T=60        T=72

**Two spiral galaxies collide and tear each other apart in this simulation by astronomer Christopher Mihos.**

It can often be very helpful to see a picture of what these equations might mean. For example, if we are studying an atomic interaction that takes place in femtoseconds, we can expand that tiniest of intervals by creating an animation that shows us what is happening at a rate of speed we can relate to, the rate at which our perception operates.

The description of the collapse of the star at the beginning of this book, while it takes far less than a second in real time, can be viewed as a slowly evolving event so that none of the details are missed.

The same is true for extremely long spans of time. Astronomers often study movements of galaxies across space. And as galaxies move, they can and do collide. We could see this with our own eyes in the skies above. But to understand what will eventually happen to these crashing galaxies, we would need to watch for perhaps 100 million years. In this case, visualization on the computer allows us to compress the time so the entire event takes place in a few minutes or hours.

## BEYOND SPACE, TOO

Just as our perception of time is limited for both the very short and the very long time span, so is our ability to perceive the unimaginably big and the incredibly small. With our egg example, we explored the world of the truly small. Now let's explore the other extreme.

We, as humans, experience and perceive the world in relation to our own size. Because of this, our ability to see and understand things, as distances and sizes get truly big, becomes less and less reliable.

It's fairly easy, for example, for us to picture something as big as a room in our house, or even something as big as our house. It's easy because it's familiar and closely related to our physical selves. It's also not that hard to think about the length of one mile. We might envision it as the distance from home to the bus stop. Or we can picture it, perhaps, as the land we cross, or the time and effort it takes to get there.

Come and browse the Moon. NASA has created a visualization tool with which the user can explore the latest data about the Moon. One image, with Earth in the background, shows the distribution of gravitational forces on the back side of the Moon. The other shows concentrations of hydrogen, and thus water, below the surface at the Moon's north pole.

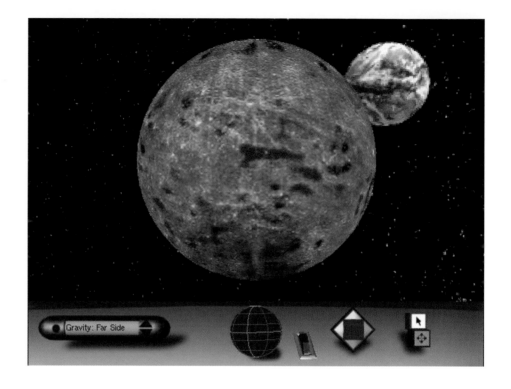

Gravity: Far Side

But what happens when we start to talk about the nearly 240,000-mile (385,000-kilometer) distance to the Moon, the 93 million miles (150 million kilometers) to the Sun, or even a single light-year. One light-year doesn't sound that big. After all, it's just one. How big can it be?

Since light moves at about 186,000 miles (300,000 kilometers) per second, we need to multiply that by 60 to calculate how far it goes in a minute, by 60 again to make an hour, then multiply that

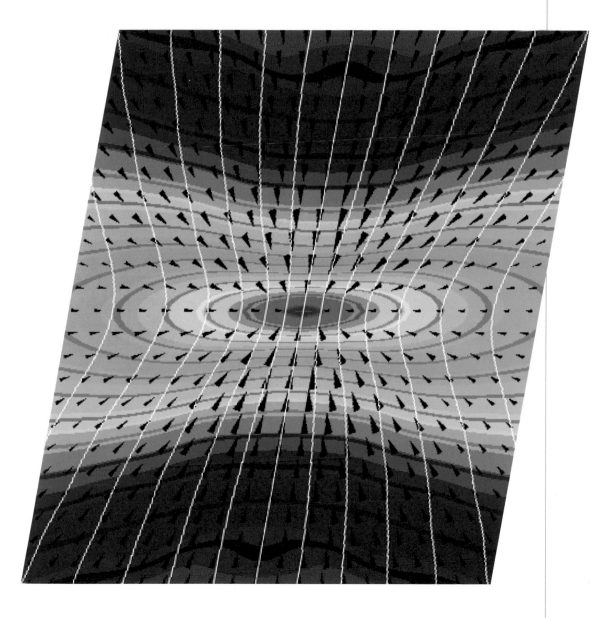

This 2-D visualization charts the lines of force in an interstellar dust cloud that lead to the formation of a new star.

number by 24 to reach a whole day, and finally multiply that number by 365 to make up one year. The total comes to more than 5 trillion miles (8 trillion kilometers). And the amazing thing is, the known universe is billions of light-years across! This is truly an unimaginable distance. However, even this can be brought down to our size by the computer, using scientific visualization, so we can relate directly to its immensity.

The colliding galaxies mentioned earlier make a good example. Each galaxy could easily span 500,000 light-years, a distance you can't exactly envision, like the distance to the bus stop. But when galaxies are reduced to animations on computer screens, scientists can easily see what is happening. They can perhaps even manipulate the galaxies with a mouse, changing everything from the size and number of the stars in each galaxy, to the speed with which they are colliding, thus providing important information that would otherwise be impossible for our brains to perceive.

## MY HEAD'S GOING TO EXPLODE!

It is this taming of the impossible that scientific visualization does so well. Have you ever had so many thoughts in your head that it feels like your head might just explode? Your problem is one that scientists have to deal with all the time: too much information. Some problems are so complex that it is impossible to keep all their components in your head.

Weather prediction, for example, seems like it should be easy: You go outside, look at the sky, test the wind, maybe make a few phone calls to find out what's going on a little farther away than you can see, and then make your guess. The fact is, for someone with experience, this may work for very short-term predictions. But for anything longer than a day or so, there are too many things to consider. What if you wanted to predict whether it would be sunny and warm for the big game two weeks from today? What would you have to consider? Potentially, millions of things.

To name just a few, you would have to know where the low- and high-pressure systems currently are, where these systems are moving and why, and how fast they are going. You might also need to know whether any new storm systems could form soon and interfere with the current weather pattern. To know this, you might also need to know ocean-current temperatures from as far away as the equator, which in turn could be affected by volcanic eruptions throwing ash in the air, or even sunspots changing the amount of solar energy reaching the earth's surface.

**Thunderstorms can be both exciting and destructive. Here scientists have simulated an intense storm racing across the plains of Oklahoma.**

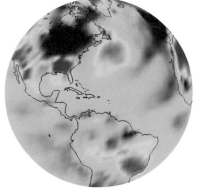

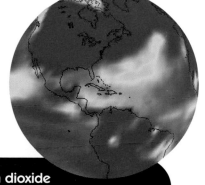

**Can the release of carbon dioxide raise the temperature of the planet? These images from a climate visualization seem to indicate that it can. After 120 years most of the cooler blues have been replaced by oranges and reds, indicating a hotter time for us all if we don't begin to curb carbon dioxide emissions.**

33

Knowing just one of these things precisely would require a huge amount of data, taken from ocean buoys, satellites, weather planes, and meteorological stations around the globe. And even if you could obtain all this information, you would still have to understand how it all fits together: how the sunspots affect ocean temperature, how that in turn affects moisture evaporation and storm formation, and so on. It is impossible for any person to handle such information without help.

To remedy this situation, atmospheric scientists have developed huge weather visualization and simulation programs that can be run on computers. These programs are models of how scientists think the world's weather behaves. They can use real data collected from all over the planet and then actually see on the computer screen what the weather might do.

Scientists can also run experiments that test what might happen if certain conditions start to change. For example, if the temperature of the oceans rose a degree or more due to global warming, some simulations predict radical changes to the world's weather, perhaps turning many fertile areas into deserts.

This ability to test different "what if" possibilities is one of the most powerful aspects of visualization systems. It also allows scientists to determine which factors, like ocean temperatures or jetstream flows, are important in a complex system like the weather. Scientists have discovered often surprising results that would normally go undetected without the use of visualization.

## December 1997 SSM/I Water Vapor
### Schluessel Algorithm

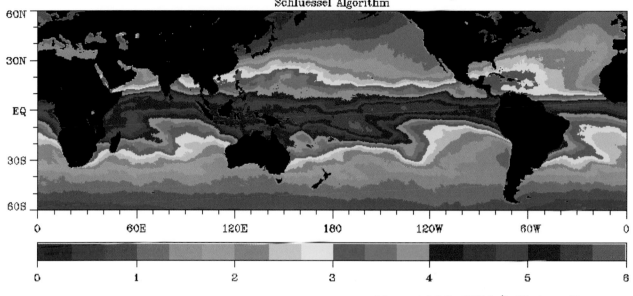

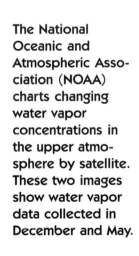

The National Oceanic and Atmospheric Association (NOAA) charts changing water vapor concentrations in the upper atmosphere by satellite. These two images show water vapor data collected in December and May.

## May 1998 SSM/I Water Vapor
### Schluessel Algorithm

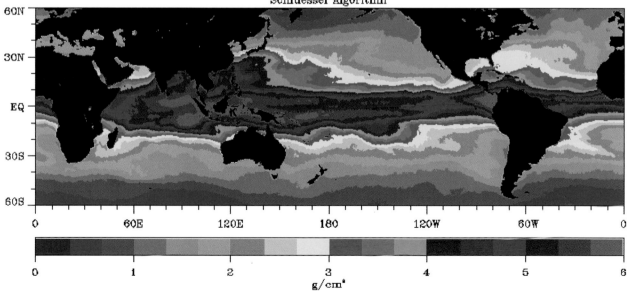

$g/cm^2$

## The Butterfly Effect

The global weather pattern was one of the first truly complex systems to be visualized on a computer. In 1961 a meteorologist at Massachusetts Institute of Technology (MIT), Dr. Edward Lorenz, was running a weather-simulation program that fed the results onto a Teletype machine (which worked similarly to a typewriter or printer) as it progressed. There were no PC's or even computer monitors on the desktop at that time, so data visualizations had to be printed out on paper.

In the middle of the simulation Lorenz had to stop the program. When he came back, he started it up again with slightly different data. After running the program for a while he noticed that something odd was happening in the printout. The weather pattern he had expected had become something completely different.

He traced the problem to the very small change he had input when he restarted the program. He had entered 0.506 instead of 0.506127. The difference was very small but had made such a change in his results, that he likened it to "a butterfly fluttering its wings in Peking, changing storm patterns in New York months later."

He discovered that even minor causes can have major effects on systems both complex and simple. This led to the creation of a whole new branch of mathematics called Chaos Theory, from which fractals (mentioned in the sidebar on page12) were born.

36

Fractals such as this one are mathematical equations that repeat infinitely. If you were to "go inside" this image and get a close-up of any of the smaller wormlike tendrils, you would notice that it looks very much like the larger fractal. The facing page may look like a field of flowers, but this, too, is actually a picture of a mathematical equation.

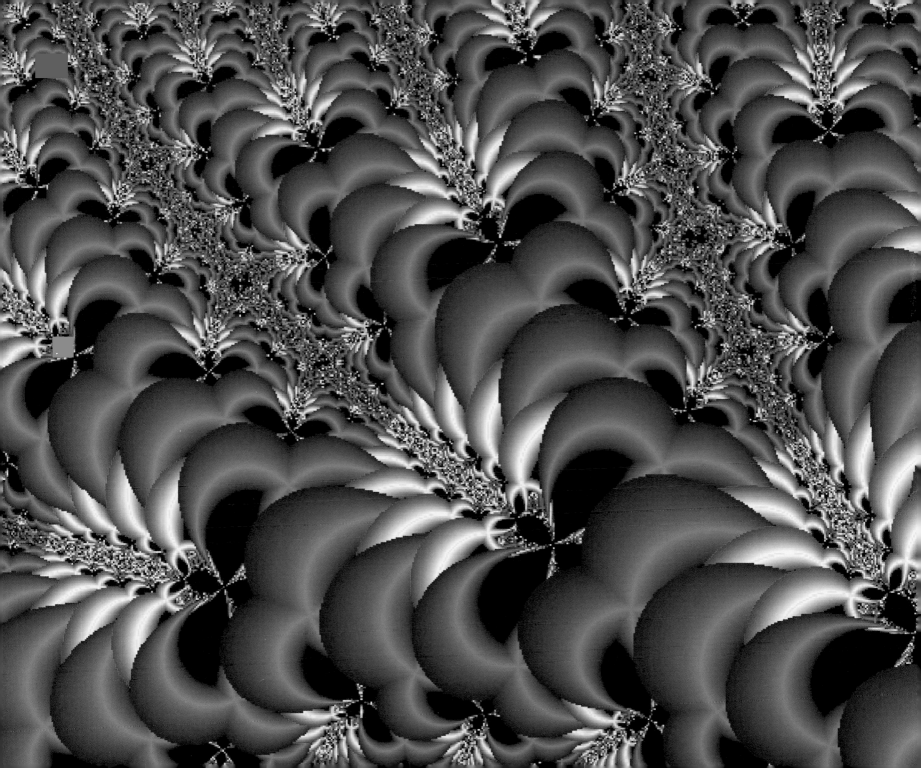

So far, most of the visualizations we have explored have been non-living systems. Not so long ago, the only way to see what was going on inside a living system was to perform surgery on a living creature. Doctors needed to open up a person or animal to look at what was going on.

But what if doctors needed to look at the heart from more than one angle—from both the front and the back? Or what if they wanted to check the health of a growing fetus without the risk of endangering the pregnancy? And what if doctors needed to see how a person's brain was functioning after having a stroke?

Surgery would be too dangerous in most such cases, and some, like the brain example, would not tell doctors anything. Fortunately,

**Here are two stunning PET scan sequences. Like the MRI scan shown earlier they show slices of the brain, but this time from top to bottom. The first set of images are of a healthy brain. The second set contains a tumor, which you can start to see in the second row. It is the bright spot on the right side of the brain.**

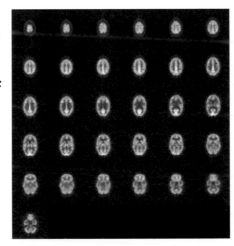
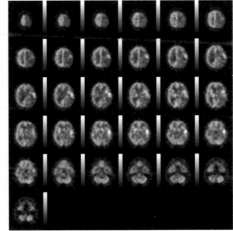

an explosion of imaging technologies now allows doctors to see inside a patient without the trauma of surgery.

There are MRI scanners, as we saw earlier, as well as ultrasound imaging devices, X-ray transmission computed tomography (CT) scanners, and positron emission tomography (PET) scanners, to name a few.

Ultrasound scanners are commonly used to give a fetus a health checkup before it is born, and to find out what sex the baby will be. It is likely that many of you were scanned in this way. Do you remember the sound?

Actually, you couldn't, even if you wanted to. Ultrasound uses extremely high-frequency sound waves that are way above the normal hearing range for humans. These high-energy sound waves are beamed through the skin of the mother's abdomen and then bounced off the fetus inside the womb. The reflecting waves are read by sensors, and a picture is created by a computer. It functions just like the radar used in planes or boats but at much lower energy levels.

Ultrasound imaging is also used to sense many other things as well, such as beating hearts, to test for irregularities that might indicate heart problems, or blood flowing through veins and arteries. By imaging the blood vessels themselves, a doctor can see if there are any restrictions that could lead to a heart attack.

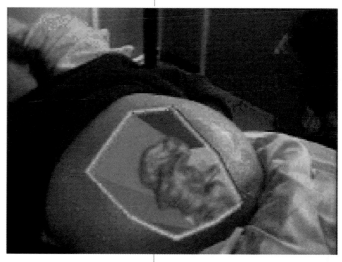

**A 3-D ultra-sound picture of a fetus inside the womb. The image is overlaid on the pregnant mother's abdomen, allowing the doctor to view just how well the fetus is developing.**

Scientists studying the behavior of sound waves use a computer to visualize sonic waves passing through a fluid and hitting a cylinder. Note what is called the standing wave pattern inside the cylinder. This pattern shows the natural vibrations of the cylinder itself.

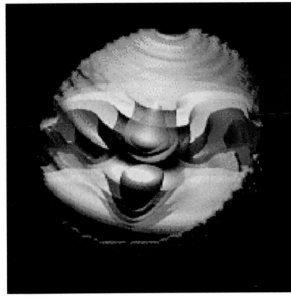

**This image shows the movement inside a kidney stone being bombarded by ultrasound. By understanding the movement inside the stone, doctors can more easily tailor necessary ultrasound treatments to break it up.**

We saw MRI scanners in action at the beginning of this book. CT scans are similar to MRIs, except that CT scans use X-ray slices taken from several different angles, instead of magnetic fields. Since X rays are used, CT scans are particularly good for looking at the harder, denser structures of the body like bones and heavier muscles. The results are much like those from the MRI. If desired, a computer can assemble the CT image slices into a solid image that a doctor can then examine.

PET scans, however, have added a whole new dimension to biological imaging. They allow doctors to image some of the inner-most biochemical processes of the body and brain in action.

## Can I Please Have My PET Scanned?

PET scanners are particularly interesting because they have provided the first detailed look at the biochemical processes of the body. They show, in effect, the cells of the body in action.

Here's how it works. A patient lying on a movable bed, as in the MRI example, is given an injection of a nontoxic radioactive chemical solution that will release positrons. Positrons are atomic particles that are positively charged, while electrons are particles of equivalent size that are negatively charged.

The solution travels through the patient's circulatory system to the area that the doctor wishes to image, such as the brain. The chemical is then used by the cells in the brain and in the process releases its positrons. These fly off from the nucleus and collide with nearby electrons. Each collision gives off energy that can be read by sensors surrounding the patient.

The data gathered by the sensors are then assembled into an image slice that is updated over time. Thus the doctor can watch as the chemical arrives in the brain and observe the behavior of the cells. The images will continue to be updated until all the positrons from the solution have been emitted.

While considerable research is being done to create 3-dimensional PET images, most PET scans currently provide only a single slice image from the area of the body being studied.

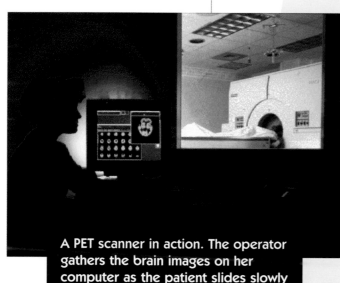

A PET scanner in action. The operator gathers the brain images on her computer as the patient slides slowly through the hoop of sensors.

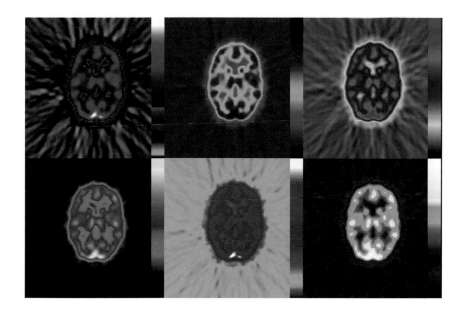

This collection of PET scans shows how useful color can be to bring out different features of the brain. The scan is the same throughout; only the colors have changed.

Among other things, PET scans have been used to study blood flow in the heart after heart attacks. They can help surgeons spot the damaged areas of the heart that could possibly be revived through what is called revascularization, or the growing or grafting of new blood vessels onto the damaged tissue.

PET scans have also been used to study both normal and abnormal brain function, giving scientists a new way to analyze mental disorders like Parkinson's and Alzheimer's diseases.

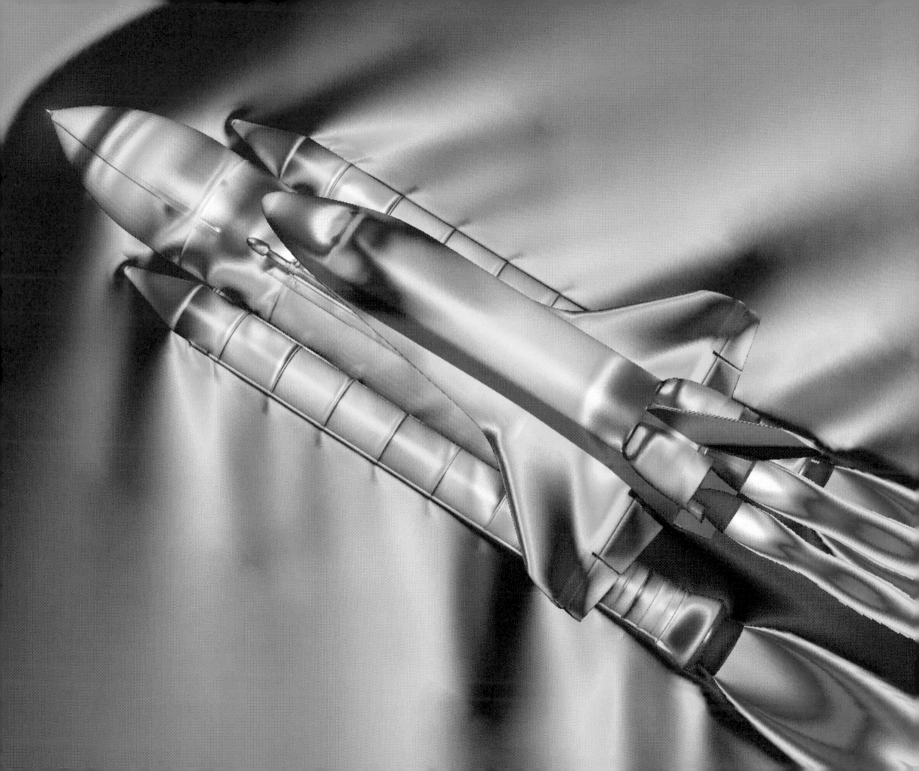

## IT'S MORE THAN JUST SEEING

Scientific visualization is much more than just seeing more clearly. Making images from complex data is certainly at the heart of this science, but what it provides is so much greater than just cool pictures.

It is really about perception: the ability not only to see but also to grasp and understand. If we understand a problem, then it becomes much easier to find a solution. For example, if scientists can see exactly how a particular cell reacts to a virus, they can design a new drug that can effectively block what that virus does. Without this visual understanding, the solution is much more difficult to find.

And beyond understanding, scientific visualization is also about extending the imagination. It allows us to create new scientific theories and test them on the computer until they match what we observe in the real world. It permits us to take complex data from the real world and bring it all together so we can see how our world works as a whole, and thus realize how each of us affects everyone else on the planet.

As a tool for expanding our awareness and guiding our discovery of who we are and where we fit in the universe, scientific visualization has no equal.

**An image of the Space Shuttle, showing the various forces that build up along its surface as it hurtles upward through the atmosphere.**

45

# RESOURCES

There are many sites on the Web that contain information about scientific visualization. Get out there and explore with the aid of your favorite internet search engine. Here are some sites to get you started.

California Institute of Technology, Computer Graphics Research   www.gg.caltech.edu

University of Colorado, Center for Human Simulation   www.uchsc.edu/sm/chs

University of Bath, UK, Physics Department   www.bath.ac.uk/Departments/Physics/groups/acoustics

Surgical Planning Laboratory, Brigham & Women's Hospital splweb.bwh.harvard.edu:8000/

University of Buffalo, Department of Nuclear Medicine   www.nucmed.buffalo.edu/

National Center for Supercomputer Applications   www.ncsa.uiuc.edu/

US Army Corp of Engineers, Construction Research Labs, Geographic Resources Analysis Support System   pandora.cecer.army.mil/grass/

National Oceanic and Atmospheric Administration (NOAA)   www.noaa.gov/

Lawrence Livermore National Labs, Scientific Visualization Group   www.llnl.gov/graphics

Los Alamos Labs, Advanced Computing Laboratory   www.acl.lanl.gov

Boston University, Scientific Computing and Visualization   scv.bu.edu/

Cornell University, Cornell Theory Center   www.tc.cornell.edu/

University of Chicago, Electronic Visualization Lab   www.evl.uic.edu

Pittsburgh Supercomputing Center   www.psc.edu/

# INDEX

DISCARD